# THE COLORING B
# JEWISH SYMBOLS

M.G. ANTHONY WITH FOREWORD BY AARON KLEIN

A POST HILL PRESS BOOK

The Coloring Book of Jewish Symbols
© 2016 by Post Hill Press
All Rights Reserved

ISBN: 978-1-68261-191-3

Interior layout by Greg Johnson, Textbook Perfect

**Post Hill**
PRESS
**Post Hill Press**
posthillpress.com

Published in the United States of America

1 2 3 4 5 6 7 8 9 10

# FOREWORD

This is not just any coloring book. It is a cathartic experience intended to take you on a meaningful journey utilizing five key symbols.

As an American living in Israel for the past ten years, the word "**Shalom**" has significant meaning for me. I personally use the word several times per day in routine conversation. The Hebrew word is commonly utilized as a salutation meaning "hello" and "goodbye," but it also means "peace." Perhaps Shalom's true meaning, however, can be divined from its Hebrew root, *Shaleim*, which means "complete," indicating that without peace there can be no completeness. As you complete the Shalom section of the coloring book, perhaps try to drown out all the noise around you and allow this expedition to bring you some inner peace.

The **Shofar** is not simply a rams' horn that is blown in synagogues on Rosh Hashanah to signify the beginning of the new year, the day that commemorates the creation of the world. Its sound and symbolism are meant to penetrate our souls, to arouse within us a spirit of repentance, to drive us to use our lives as a force for good in the world around us. The sound reminds me of the sweetness that accompanies the Jewish New Year—the apple dipped in honey on Rosh Hashanah. That same sweetness should ensconce our internal new year, the awakening that comes with the blast of the Shofar.

The **Hamsa** amulet is a talisman utilized by some in Judaism and other religions to protect against the "evil eye," meaning negative energy in the universe. The name is derived from the Hebrew word *Hamesh*, which means "five," as in the five fingers on the hand. Some see it as representing the hand of Moses raised to ensure success in battle, while others say it signifies the five books of the Torah. The Hamsa is clearly meant to signify protection in a chaotic universe.

The Hebrew word "**Chai**" means "living" or "alive;" it signifies the life force that drives us, that compels us to keep going. And there are few symbols as lively as the **Star of David**, which has become the emblem of Judaism and modern Jewish identity. And, of course, the Star of David adorns the Israeli flag, the banner of the Holy Land, the one true democracy in the Middle East, the only nation in the region where human life is fully respected, where people from all religions are free to live, worship, and prosper.

*Aaron Klein*

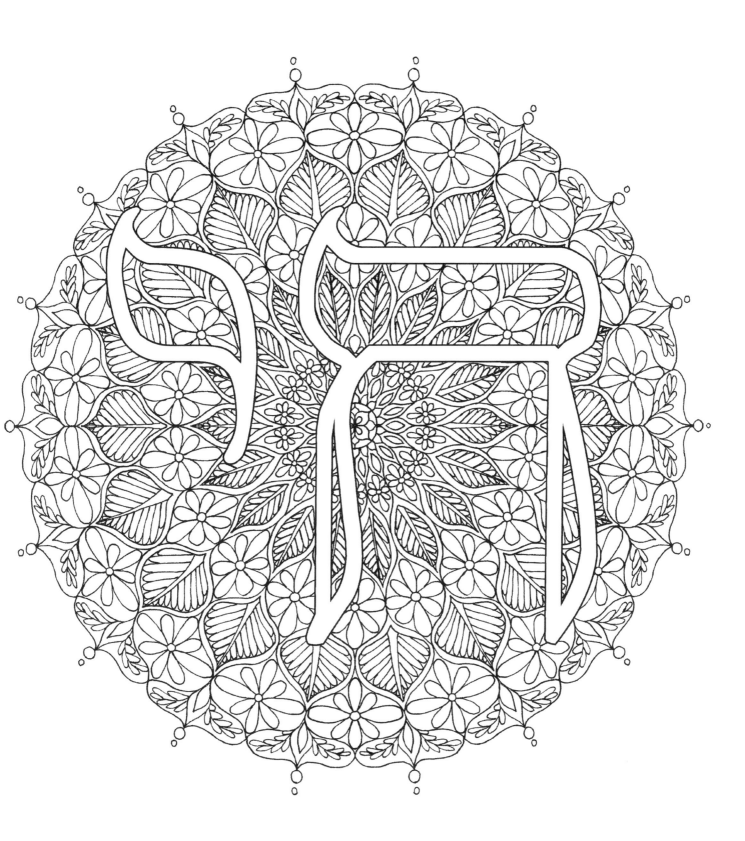